The *STAR WARS*
Question & Answer Book About
COMPUTERS

The STAR WARS Question & Answer Book About COMPUTERS

By **Fred D'Ignazio**
Illustrated by **Ken Barr**

RUN

RANDOM HOUSE

For Catie and Eric,
who love robots and computers

Photograph and illustration credits: Amdahl Corp., 15; APL Photograph/Johns Hopkins University, 51 (top); Apple Computer Inc., 21, 44, 51 (bottom); AT&T Photo/Graphics Center, 8; Ken Barr, cover, 5, 9, 10, 15, 18, 24, 29, 31, 33, 35, 37, 41, 43, 47, 48 (bottom), 50 (left), 55, 56, 60; Battelle-Northwest Photography, 48 (top); Bell Laboratories, 14 (bottom), 16, 17, 34, 52, 59; Heath Co., 45; International Business Machines Corporation, 25, 26, 27, 28, 50 (right); International Telephone and Telegraph Corporation, 13; © 1981 Eric Kroll/Taurus Photos, 46 (bottom); © 1980 Lucasfilm Ltd. (LFL), 46 (top); Mattel, 19; NASA, 33, 53, 54; Odyssey Products–N.A.P. Consumer Electronics Corp., 20; A. Owczarzak/Taurus Photos, 14 (top); Dr. Melvin L. Prueitt, Los Alamos National Laboratory, 22; L.L.T. Rhodes/Taurus Photos, 23; Martin M. Rotker/Taurus Photos, 58; James Somers/Taurus Photos, 11; Western Electric, 12.

Library of Congress Cataloging in Publication Data:
D'Ignazio, Fred. The Star Wars question and answer book about computers.
SUMMARY: Question-and-answer format presents information on how computers work, what their insides are like, and the wide variety of uses to which they have been put today—inside robots, in games, and inside human bodies.
1. Computers—Juvenile literature. 2. Electronic data processing—Juvenile literature. 3. Automation—Juvenile literature.
[1. Computers. 2. Questions and answers] I. Title. QA76.23.D53   1983   001.64   82–19030 ISBN: 0-394-85686-4 (trade); 0-394-95686-9 (lib. bdg.)

Manufactured in the United States of America   2 3 4 5 6 7 8 9 0

INTRODUCTION

The *Star Wars* movies introduce you to worlds in outer space. Now R2-D2 is going to take you on a journey to a different kind of world. It isn't out past the moon, or out among the stars and galaxies. It is right here on earth. It is all around you. It is the world of the computer.

R2-D2 is the perfect guide. He is a robotdroid and is actually controlled by a computer himself. If you have seen the *Star Wars* movies, you are aware that he is also a computer expert. R2-D2's computer gives him the ability to think fast and help his human friends.

In this book R2-D2 and C-3PO will take you on a trip to two different computer worlds. The first is our familiar, everyday world. In it computers are used inside washing machines, cars, calculators, televisions, and electronic games. There is also a world inside the computer. This world is very, very tiny. It is different from the familiar world we know. It is a strange world, yet very beautiful.

R2-D2 and C-3PO will also show you computers that go into space and deep under the sea. You will see computers that act as brains to working robots. You will meet computers that play games and make movies. R2-D2 will even show you how you can teach a computer and make it obey you.

WHAT IS A COMPUTER?

What Is a Computer?

A computer is a machine that obeys a list of commands stored in its memory. You can give the computer these commands by typing them on an electronic typewriter wired to the computer. The commands are stored in the computer's memory as tiny charges of electricity.

What Can a Computer Do?

It all depends on what you tell the computer to do. The computer is usually built inside another machine. It acts as a brain to control the machine. You give the brain its orders. You can order it to remember the birthdays of all your family members and friends. You can order it to do arithmetic and add up lots of big numbers. You can order it to play "Yankee Doodle," control a pet robot, battle you in an exciting game, or, if the computer is built into a dishwasher, wash your family's dishes.

What Are Computers Good at Doing?

Computers are good at arithmetic, making decisions, and controlling other machines, including robots, digital watches, and space shuttles. Computers are also good at playing games, making artificial speech and music, and storing pictures. Computers are especially good at remembering information, then showing it to you when you give them the right command.

A computer system in action.

What Are Computers Not Good at Doing?

Computers are not especially good at acting like real creatures—including toads, dogs, and human beings. But they are learning. Computers are being taught to see, hear, touch, smell, and move. They are also being taught to think, learn, and be creative. But their progress is slow. According to scientists, in terms of thinking on their own, computers are now at the level of a bug—a spider or a gnat.

Are Computers Smart?

They can be. However, when a computer is first built, it can do nothing—until you teach it. You teach it to do things by giving it commands in its special language. How smart it becomes depends on how good a teacher you are. Some people are very good computer teachers. They are teaching computers to play chess, read a newspaper, discover new oil deposits underground, solve complicated math problems, and diagnose sick people's infections. Computer teachers are showing computers how to do things that would be considered smart if people did them.

Are Computers Smarter Than People?

No. Computers can act smarter than people only in very narrow, specialized ways. For example, a computer may soon be the world chess champion. And a computer can recall an encyclopedia full of facts in just a couple of seconds.

On the other hand, computers might take minutes or hours to do something that would be simple for you. For example, imagine that you and a computerized robot were in the same room. Imagine that your goal was to find a yellow tennis ball underneath a coffee table. Who could find the ball first, you or the robot? The answer is you! You could have the ball in your hand before the robot even figured out what a ball looked like.

What Makes Computers Seem So Smart?

Three things: speed, memory, and make-believe. One, computers are very fast. Some computers can add a million numbers in less than a second. Two, computers have huge memories. Some computers know the name of every star in the sky. Other computers know the name of every man, woman, and child in America. Three, computers are good pretenders. Depending on what orders you give them, computers can pretend to be anything in the world. You can teach a computer to act like a watch and tell time or act like a spaceship flying to Venus or Mars.

THE WORLD INSIDE THE COMPUTER

What Is the World Inside the Computer?

The world inside the computer is made up of the little wires, pathways, and tunnels that carry information. The information is in the form of electricity.

Where Is the World Inside the Computer?

Pretend that you are playing with a computer game and suddenly an evil dragon appears and blasts your computer with his fiery breath. The plastic and metal shell of the computer melts away. All that is left are the tiny wires, pathways, and tunnels inside. This is the world inside the computer.

What Does the World Inside the Computer Look Like?

The dragon winks at you, then disappears. Amazed, you lean over your computer, reach inside, and pick up what looks like a green plastic card. On the card are lots of little black tiles. Inside these tiles are the computer's miniature pathways and tunnels—*millions* of them!

The pathways and tunnels are very, very small. To see them you would need a microscope. Or else you would need to become so tiny that a snowflake would seem as big as a house, a grain of sand would seem like a mountain.

If you could shrink down to the size of a germ and dive into the computer, you would see all the pathways and tunnels spilling across the computer's world like tangled spaghetti noodles.

Miniature pathways and tunnels of a microchip.

What Do the Pathways Look Like?

The pathways swoop and dive, overlap and intersect. If you see them all together through a microscope, they don't look like pathways and tunnels. They look more like a city with tall buildings; dark, narrow alleys; wide streets; trees; railroad tracks; and racetracks.

What Do the Pathways Do?

They carry a computer's information and commands in the form of lightning-fast pulses of electricity.

How Do the Pathways Work?

All pathways inside the computer either carry or store an electrical charge. The pathways that store charges are called the computer's memory. The pathways that guide charges and turn them on and off are part of the computer's brain. The simplest pathways are known as *transistors*.

What Is a Transistor?

A transistor is an electronic device that can dramatically increase an electrical charge. The first one was invented by three scientists at Bell Laboratories in 1947.

Transistors have three jobs. They act as magnifying glasses and make small electrical charges large. (They can also make large charges shrink into small charges.) They act as light switches and turn charges on and off. And they act as traffic cops and route the flow of traffic (electrical charges) through the computer.

A transistor is made of two pathways. The pathways crisscross each other but don't touch. One pathway passes above the other like a bridge over a stream. The charges of electricity flow from one pathway to another through a special material. The special material used in most transistors is *silicon*.

First transistor.

What Is Silicon?

Silicon is an *element*. Elements are the building blocks of the universe. Everything in the universe—you, a rock, a plant, a planet, or a star—is made from a little more than one hundred elements. Oxygen is an element. Iron is an element. Mercury is an element. And silicon is one too.

Like oxygen, silicon is one of the most abundant elements on earth. Millions of tons of silicon are mixed in with the sand on the earth's beaches. When you walk along the beach on a sunny day, you can see tiny silicon crystals sparkling in the sand.

Why Are Transistors Made of Silicon?

Silicon is a material that can increase an electrical charge. There are other materials that do the same thing, but silicon is abundant and inexpensive. If you look at silicon under a microscope, you see that it is made of tiny crystals, like glass squares and triangles all glued together.

Transistor pathways are built in silicon, like tunnels, channels, bridges, and overpasses. Under certain conditions electrical charges will "jump" across the silicon crystals. Also, depending on the way the pathways are built, an electrical charge that jumps across the silicon can be magnified or shrunk, turned on or off.

Each charge—big or little—represents one unit of information. Hundreds, thousands, even millions of these charges are strung together across a computer's silicon transistors like beads on a necklace. This is how all information is guided, routed, stored, and processed inside the computer.

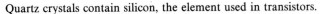

Quartz crystals contain silicon, the element used in transistors.

How Do Transistors Carry Information?

By working together in groups. A single transistor can only magnify a charge, shrink a charge, turn it on or off, or route it to another transistor. But transistors can be combined into *circuits* that perform more interesting jobs. Most circuits (many transistors working together) are either *memory* circuits or *logic* circuits. Memory circuits store information in the form of charges. Logic circuits enable a computer to add two numbers. They enable a computer to make decisions and add letters together to make new words.

The simplest circuits (of only a few transistors) are combined with one another to form more complex circuits, like small streams feeding into giant rivers. The most complex circuits make up the computer's brain. They are composed of thousands or millions of transistors. A computer's brain can solve difficult math problems, predict the weather, play music, or steer a robot spaceship across the solar system.

Circuit board.

Computer chip on a postage stamp.

How Big Is the Computer's Brain?

It takes hundreds of thousands of transistors to make just one computer brain. Yet the brain is so tiny that it can fit on a crystal flake of silicon small enough to fit on a postage stamp.

Why Did Computer Brains Get So Small?

In the 1940s, when the first computers were built, they were as big as a brontosaurus. Their wires were as thick as jungle snakes. But scientists wanted computers to be small so that they could fit on board rocket ships and be launched into space. Military generals wanted small, fast computers that would fit inside military weapons like guided missiles and jet fighters. Businesspeople wanted computers to run faster, store more information, and cost less money. These three groups (scientists, generals, and businesspeople) worked together to make computers smaller, lighter, faster, cheaper, and more reliable.

The Amdahl 470 supercomputer can process tens of millions of commands in a single second.

How Did Computer Transistors Change in Size?

All computers are made from parts that carry, route, or store electrical charges. But these parts were not always transistors. In the 1940s and early 1950s they were big, hot vacuum tubes the size of pickles. In the mid-1950s the first computers made out of transistors were built. Each transistor was about the size of the eraser on the tip of a pencil.

In the early 1960s scientists found a way to shrink transistors. First they took a picture of all the transistors in a memory or logic circuit. Then they reduced the picture and "printed" it on a sliver of silicon thinner than a human hair. Each piece of silicon was the size of a person's fingernail and was called a *chip*. The whole circuit, made of dozens of transistors, fit on the chip. Each transistor had shrunk to the size of a freckle, or even smaller.

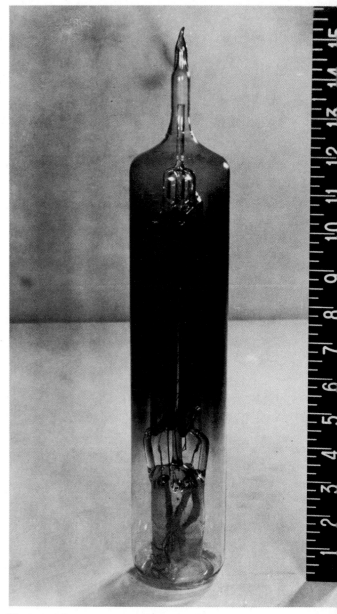

Vacuum tube.

Can a Whole Computer Fit on a Chip?

Yes, some recent computers fit on a single chip. But this was not true in the early days of computers. Even as late as the 1960s it took hundreds of chips, wired together, to make a computer. But scientists kept finding new ways to shrink transistors and squeeze more and more on a chip. Finally in 1969, Ted Hoff, of Intel Corporation in Santa Clara, California, managed to fit an entire computer brain on a single chip. A few years later Intel and other companies had built entire computers—with memories, brains, and other parts—all on a single chip.

Are Computers Still Shrinking?

No. New computer chips are the same size as the old ones. But scientists are finding new ways to shrink the chip pathways and transistors. This lets scientists squeeze more and more pathways and transistors onto a single chip.

Today, in the mid-1980s, scientists have built computers on a chip filled with over a million miniature transistors. These computers cost only pennies to make and run on a penlight battery. Yet they are faster and can remember more information than the million-dollar computers of only thirty years ago. The new computers could fit on the tip of your tongue. The old computers were the size of your school gym.

How Do You Use a Computer Chip?

To use a computer chip you need to connect it to a typewriter and a television screen.

You use a computer by typing a command on a typewriter wired to the computer chip. The command you type turns into electrical charges that flash over the wires. The charges start out on rope-sized wires connected to the typewriter. Then they move to wires the size of strings, then threads. Then they get even smaller, until they are the tiny pathways on a silicon chip.

For example, if you want the computer to add the numbers 50 and 25, you might type the following command: PRINT 50 + 25. The command would be converted into a string of electrical charges that would flow along the wires to the computer brain chip. The brain would obey the command. It would send the answer back over the wires to your TV. The answer, 75, would appear on the TV screen.

On a typewriter connected to the computer, the operator enters his command, which is then converted into electrical charges and obeyed by the computer.

COMPUTER GAMES

What Is a Computer Game?
A computer game is any game wired to a computer chip. There are arcade games, home video (TV) games, hand-held games, board games, pocket games, and wristwatch games.

Where Is the Game Computer Chip Located?
The computer chip is hidden inside the game. A computer game might have only a single chip or up to dozens of memory and brain chips.

What Does the Brain Chip Do?

The brain chip has many important jobs. First, as the game *referee,* it explains all the game rules to you and makes sure that you follow them. Second, as the *scorekeeper,* it keeps track of how many points are scored in the game. Third, as *timekeeper,* it acts like a stopwatch and makes sure each game lasts only so long. Fourth, as game *director,* it puts pictures on the game screen and makes music, voices, and sound effects come out of the speakers. And fifth, as *opponent,* it tries lots of tricky strategies to beat you.

What Does the Memory Chip Do?

The memory chip has three major jobs. First, it stores the rules for the game. Second, it stores the game sounds and game pictures. And third, it stores the scores, penalties, and bonus points.

Simple wristwatch and hand-held computer games might have only one memory chip. Fancy arcade computer games might have dozens of memory chips and maybe even several brain chips. This is what makes the game action so fast and the pictures and sound effects so spectacular.

A computer is hidden inside of this adventure board game.

What Was the First Computer Game?

People probably began to secretly play games on computers when they were first invented, during the mid-1940s. But in the 1940s and 1950s there were only a few dozen computers in the whole world, and most people thought computers were serious machines and should only be used to solve problems for science, business, and the military.

In 1962 Steve Russell, in Cambridge, Massachusetts, invented a game called Spacewar. At first the game was a secret, especially from Steve's bosses, who owned the computer. But the game was so exciting that people started calling Steve to get copies of Spacewar to play on their computers. Pretty soon computers all over the country were playing Spacewar with human beings.

19

What Was the First Arcade Computer Game?

In 1971 Nolan Bushnell took an electronic game he invented to a bar in Sunnyvale, California. The game was a lot like Ping-Pong. A little blip of light bounced back and forth across a TV screen. On opposite sides of the screen human players could control small blocks of light called paddles. When the blip of light hit a paddle, it bounced back to the other player's side. If it missed, it disappeared from the screen, and the player who last hit the blip scored a point. Bushnell called his game Pong, and it became so successful that it made Bushnell a millionaire. Bushnell used his millions to found a computer-game company. He named the company Atari. Today Atari is the world's largest manufacturer of electronic games.

What Was the First Home Video Game?

Ralph Baer spent 1970 and 1971 in his workshop trying to figure out ways to connect the new computer chips to his TV set so he could play games. He succeeded. In late 1971 he took his invention to Magnavox, a large U.S. electronics company. Magnavox bought the rights to Ralph's invention and, in 1972, introduced Odyssey, the world's first commercial home video game.

What Was the First Hand-Held Computer Game?

The first hand-held game was Auto-Race, made by Mattel Electronics in 1977. There are now over five hundred different kinds of hand-held games.

This computerized adventure board game creates cartoon images and sound effects.

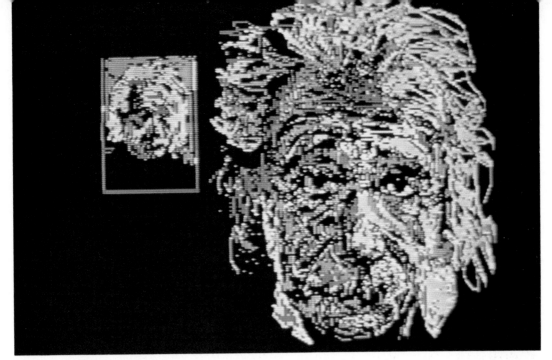

Block art of Albert Einstein.

How Do Computers Make Game Pictures?

There are two popular techniques: coloring in the blocks and "string art."

What Is the Coloring-in-the-Block Technique?

You can understand this technique by looking at a piece of graph paper, which you can buy or make. (You can make it by crisscrossing a blank page with lots of horizontal [sideways] lines and vertical [up-and-down] lines.)

Look at the paper. Note all the little squares, or boxes. Now get some crayons or markers and color in the boxes to make a picture. Try a house, a horse, a spaceship, or a monster.

A computer game draws pictures the same way. The computer's TV screen has lots of little invisible boxes. You can teach the computer to color in each of these boxes to make a picture.

How Does the Computer Make String-Art Pictures?

Again, look at a piece of graph paper. Look at the points where the lines cross. Put your pencil on one of those points. Now draw a straight line to any other point on the page. Now do it again. Now try to draw a picture this way.

Some computers have TV screens with rows of points instead of rows of boxes. You can teach these computers to connect the points with straight lines to draw a picture. You can even get the computer to draw circles this way by drawing lots and lots of tiny straight lines, each one shifted around a center point.

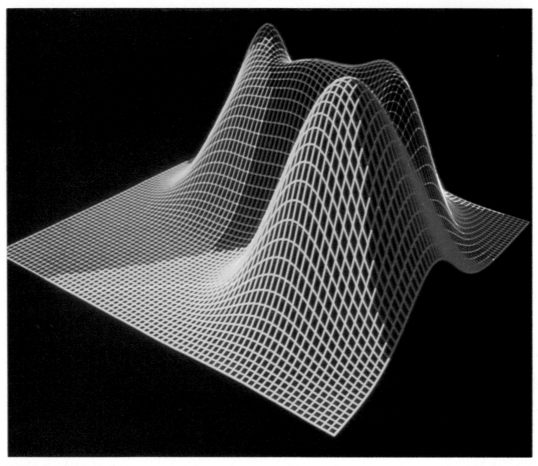
Computer graphics.

How Do Computers Make Sound Effects?

With electrical pulses, or waves. Sound is made of waves—not ocean waves made of water but floating waves made of molecules of air dancing, or vibrating, through space. We hear a sound when a wave of air bumps into our eardrum and gets it vibrating too.

Each kind of sound wave wiggles with a certain strength. One wiggles slowly and lazily, like a slithery snake. Another wiggles fast and often, like an excited puppy.

You can teach a computer to send out electrical pulses that start low, grow quickly, then shrink to almost nothing. These pulses also resemble a wave.

When the pulses strike a speaker (like on your radio or stereo), they make tiny cones in the speaker vibrate. The vibrations produce sound waves of air that look just like the electrical waves coming out of the computer.

Depending on what you make the waves look like, they will create a sound that is like a bass guitar, a kettledrum, a church organ, a person speaking, or an exploding firecracker.

How Do People Become Game Experts?

People become good at computer games with lots of practice, lots of quarters, and by *watching for patterns.* All electronic games follow patterns. For example, when a game monster or spaceship moves around the screen in the same way every time, it is following a pattern.

Computer games have patterns because the game is really a list of orders flashing through the computer's brain. There is a limited number of orders, so eventually the computer goes back to some old orders, and the game repeats itself.

Knowing when a game repeats itself is the secret to winning. If you know when an enemy spaceship or monster is coming your way, you lie low. Then you zap it when it comes around the bend. Computer-game experts are those people who know a game inside and out. They have mastered all the patterns, and they use their knowledge to pile up millions of points.

Two girls battle for points during an arcade video game of football.

THE FIRST COMPUTERS

Where Did Computers Come From?

For thousands of years people have been inventing calculating devices to help them with their arithmetic. Addition and subtraction done by hand was tiring, hard, and often full of mistakes. So someone invented the calculator—a machine that does arithmetic.

The invention of the computer grew out of the search for a new, more powerful kind of calculator. Working calculators were invented hundreds of years ago. They did not resemble the modern pocket calculator. They resembled concrete blocks and circular rulers. More recently they looked like large typewriters.

What Is the Difference Between a Calculator and a Computer?

Computers and modern electronic calculators appear to be very similar. They can do arithmetic and they are controlled by computer chip "brains." They work with numbers and obey rigid mathematical and logical rules. But a calculator works with numbers only and hasn't much memory. A calculator is a special-purpose arithmetic machine.

A computer can do arithmetic. But it can also do much more. First, it can store a huge quantity of information. Second, it can obey many more commands. Most calculators know only four commands: add, subtract, multiply, and divide. A computer might be able to obey forty commands, four hundred, or four million. It usually has a few simple commands—like JUMP, READ, and WRITE—that act as building blocks. These commands can be combined to form endless numbers of new commands.

All this makes the computer a general-purpose machine. It can be taught to imitate any other machine. It can be taught to imitate anything.

Who First Thought of the Computer?

Charles Babbage. Babbage was an eccentric English mathematician living in London in the early 1800s. Babbage began by building a "super calculator"—a machine to calculate tables of numbers perfectly.

Babbage abandoned this first machine in 1833 when he ran out of money. Then, on borrowed funds, he began to build a new machine, which he called the Analytical Engine.

Charles Babbage, English mathematician, whose work inspired computer inventors.

How Did the Analytical Engine Work?

Babbage never finished building the Analytical Engine, but his plans called for a machine that was big and heavy, made of metal wheels, gears, levers, rods, and springs, and hand-powered by turning a crank.

What Did Babbage Hope the Analytical Engine Would Do?

When finished, Babbage's machine would have done complicated arithmetic. It would have solved logical problems, made decisions, and played chess by obeying commands fed into it on stiff paper cards with holes punched in them.

Why Didn't Babbage Finish Building His Analytical Engine?

It was too complicated for the technology of his time. Babbage had imagined a machine so advanced that its parts hadn't even been invented yet. After decades of work Babbage finally abandoned his dream, convinced that he had failed.

Who Built the First Computer?

Howard Aiken. Babbage never built his computer, but many brilliant inventors learned about Babbage's work and were inspired by his ideas.

Finally, technology caught up with the inventors. In the late 1930s and early 1940s Aiken built the Mark I, the world's first modern, electric-powered computer. The Mark I was a monster. It was forty-five feet long, eight feet high, and made of a million different parts. It's been said that it sounded like "a roomful of ladies knitting with steel needles."

Aiken called the Mark I "Babbage's dream come true." When the Mark I was unveiled in 1944, Aiken said, "If Charles Babbage were alive today, I'd be out of a job."

The Mark I, developed by Howard Aiken in the late 1930s.

The Mark I was a great step forward. Yet only two years later a much more powerful computer was built. In February 1946, after thirty months of round-the-clock effort, John Mauchley and J. Presper Eckert turned on the power to ENIAC (Electronic Numerical Integrator and Calculator), the world's first *electronic* computer. The ENIAC was the granddaddy of today's modern computers.

ENIAC, the world's first electronic computer, 1946.

What's the Difference Between the ENIAC and the Mark I?

The Mark I was powered by electricity but used mechanical arms (called *relays*) to route the electricity and to carry and store information. The ENIAC used hot, glowing vacuum tubes (nineteen thousand of them!) to do the same thing. Vacuum tubes had no moving parts and were much faster than the relays. For example, the Mark I could do only two addition problems a second, but the ENIAC could do a thousand.

Are Vacuum Tubes Used in Today's Computers?

No. Vacuum tubes were fast, but they used enormous amounts of electricity. They turned computers into burning ovens that had to be constantly cooled or they would have melted. And vacuum tubes were not very reliable. Every time the ENIAC was turned on, somewhere one of its vacuum tubes burned out.

Electronic vacuum tubes, which powered the earlier computers such as the ENIAC.

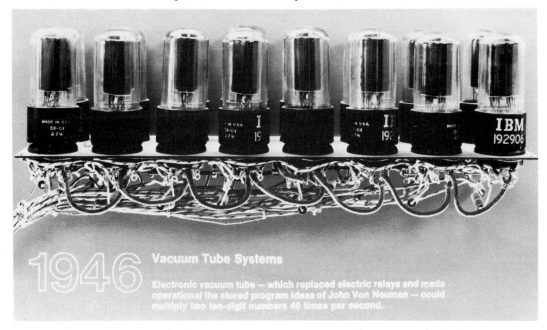

1946 Vacuum Tube Systems

Electronic vacuum tube — which replaced electric relays and made operational the stored program ideas of John Von Neuman — could multiply two ten-digit numbers 40 times per second.

What Do Modern Computers Use Instead of Vacuum Tubes?

Transistors. Two days before Christmas in 1947 a team of scientists at Bell Laboratories in New Jersey built the world's first transistor. Like the vacuum tube, it could carry, store, and route electrical signals. And the transistor was faster, cooler, more reliable, and a hundred times smaller than the vacuum tube.

What Are the Transistors in Today's Computers Like?

First of all, they have shrunk to a size so small that you need a microscope to see them. Original transistors in the 1940s were the size of paper clips. Today millions of transistors could fit in the same space.

Super-small transistors are the secret behind the revolution in computers. According to computer scientist Christopher Evans, if cars had evolved as quickly as computers, you could buy a super-deluxe Rolls-Royce today for under three dollars! It would get three million miles to the gallon. And it would be as powerful as the ocean liner *QE2*.

Did Computers Shrink Along with the Transistor?

At first, computers stayed the same size or got even bigger. On the outside they looked the same. On the inside, however, they contained thousands or millions of extra transistors. This made them many times more powerful than the first computers.

These computers were used by businesspeople, scientists, and the military. But there were people who wanted their own computers. They began to build homemade computers out of the wires and bodies of big computers that had been thrown away.

How Big Were the Homemade Computers?

The first homemade computers, made during the 1960s, were as big as your living room, or bigger. They cost thousands of dollars to build, even using second-hand parts and scrap parts.

During the 1970s, with the invention of chip-sized computer brains and memories, things changed. Using chips, hobbyists began to build whole computers that could fit on top of a desk or table. In 1975 the first computer kit was introduced. Twenty years earlier, computers cost millions of dollars and took teams of experts weeks or months to build. Now people could buy a computer for just a few hundred dollars and build it in their home in just a few days.

MODERN COMPUTERS: GIANTS AND DWARFS

What Is a Giant Computer?

A giant computer is called a *supercomputer.* A supercomputer is made of hundreds of tiny computer chips all wired together. Each chip is faster and stores more information than the room-sized computers of thirty years ago.

There are only about fifty supercomputers in the whole world. Most are used by the military, by NASA (National Aeronautics and Space Administration), by scientific laboratories, and by weathermen to help predict the world's weather.

A supercomputer is about the size of a classroom. It costs more than ten million dollars. It can obey more than twenty million commands in a single second. Its memory is enormous. In a single second it can remember any one of a trillion bits of information. And it might take a company nine months to a year to build. (By contrast, a company can build a small home computer in about forty-five minutes.)

What Is the World's Fastest Computer?

The X-MP, made by Cray Research in Minneapolis, Minnesota. The X-MP can do a billion arithmetic problems in just one second.

Why Is the X-MP So Fast?

The X-MP is so fast because it has a "fishnet" of tiny chip brains all wired together and solving different problems at the same time.

Small personal computers and supercomputers like the X-MP do arithmetic, process information, and solve problems. But they are as different as one-lane streets and superhighways. Small computers are like one-lane streets: They can obey only one command at a time and solve only one problem at a time. But the X-MP is like a superhighway with sixty-four lanes. It can obey sixty-four commands at a time and solve sixty-four problems at a time.

The two kinds of computers resemble roads in another way too. Cars on narrow, one-lane streets move slowly; cars on superhighways move fast. The same is true for small computers and supercomputers. It takes a small desk-top computer a few thousandths of a second to obey just one command. But the X-MP can obey sixty-four commands in only a few billionths of a second.

What Can You Do with a Supercomputer?

You can load information about temperatures, rainstorms, blizzards, tornadoes, and cloud patterns from all over the globe into a supercomputer and predict the world's weather.

You can enter rock formations, chemical tests, and other information about the earth's formation into a supercomputer and use it to predict where to drill for oil. Supercomputers have already saved oil companies billions of dollars by taking much of the guesswork out of oil prospecting.

How Do Supercomputers Solve Problems?

By building models. Have you ever built a model airplane or model car? Scientists use a supercomputer to build models too. They might create a model of a hurricane, a beating heart, or an orbiting satellite. But they don't build their models out of plastic and glue. They use numbers—complicated formulas of numbers.

And they run! Scientists turn these models on, speed them up, slow them down, and make them run backward. The supercomputer can translate all the numbers into cartoonlike pictures of the thing being modeled. Scientists can watch their models on the computer's color TV screen as an animated movie. For example, the computer can draw a picture of a horse. In just a few seconds scientists can watch the horse evolve over millions of years from a three-toed, doglike creature into a one-toed racehorse. Or scientists can get the computer to draw a picture of the earth. They make a computer "movie" of the earth and watch it grow over billions of years out of boulders and dirt clods being pasted and slapped together. Or doctors can get a computer to draw a picture of a person's vital organs, like the heart, lungs, and liver. In a minute the doctors can watch a person's body cope with an illness that might take weeks or years to develop normally.

What Else Can Supercomputers Do?

Supercomputers are like scientific crystal balls. They can be used to guess at things that have not yet happened. They also let scientists see things that would be impossible to see in any other way. For example, they can make "movies" of our galaxy, the Milky Way, spinning through space, the way it might look from another galaxy. They can show mathematicians what the fourth dimension might look like by drawing whirling 3-D "shadows" of boxes, bottles, and spheres that exist only in the fourth dimension.

Supercomputers are also being used to make special effects and scenes that appear in real motion pictures like the new *Star Wars* movies. But making an entire movie scene is hard, even for a super-computer. Older computers used to take a whole year just to create a scene that lasts only two and a half minutes. New supercomputers are much faster. But it still takes a supercomputer about twenty minutes to create a scene that lasts only a single second.

What Is a Dwarf Computer?

A "dwarf computer" is a small computer used in a calculator, electronic game, appliance, or home computer. Supercomputers use thousands of chips for their brain and memory. Dwarf computers use only one or two brain chips and just a few memory chips. Supercomputers are rare; dwarf computers are everywhere. They are inside our toys, calculators, digital watches, automobiles, TV sets, washing machines, microwave ovens, and electronic games. Soon they will be inside our clothes, our furniture, even our bodies.

In our clothes they could record our body temperature, pulse, respiration, and other vital signs. They could warn us if anything looked wrong. They could be embedded inside furniture, bridges, and buildings to detect too little moisture, too much stress, and other dangerous or damaging conditions. In our bodies, they could run pacemakers, hearing aids, seeing aids, artificial limbs, and artificial organs. They could even generate artificial speech for people who cannot talk.

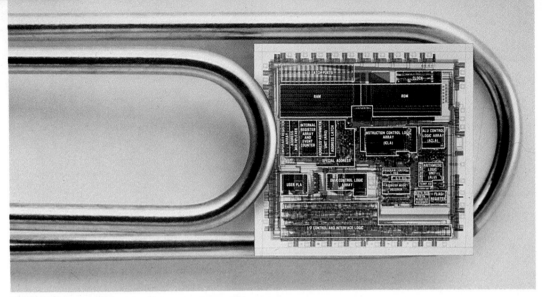

The MAC-4 one-chip computer on a paper clip.

What Is a Dwarf Computer Made Of?

A dwarf computer usually has one kind of brain chip and two kinds of memory chips. The brain chip is called a *CPU* (or Central Processing Unit). It is like a busy train station or airport. Every piece of information and every command inside the computer must be processed by the brain chip. The commands all come whizzing through one at a time; the bits of information arrive in small groups, a thousand times a second.

One kind of memory chip is known as RAM (or Random Access Memory). It is like having a pencil and an empty scratch pad when your mother gives you a list of jobs to do. As she gives you the jobs you write them all down. Then you do them. Each time the computer is given a set of tasks (called a *program*), it makes a list of these tasks in its RAM memory. Then the brain chip obeys the tasks one at a time.

The other kind of memory chip is known as ROM (or Read Only Memory). ROM is like one of your stereo records. The music is put on your record at a factory when the record is first made. You can play the music on the record, but you can't erase the music and add new music of your own. And ROM is the same way—only with orders and information instead of music. The orders and information are stored on ROM at the factory. You can't erase anything or store your own orders or information.

What Does ROM Look Like?

If you have ever played a home video game or a computer game, you have used ROM. ROM chips are packaged inside plastic game cartridges. You plug the cartridges into a home computer or video game. The game instructions are flashed from the ROM chip to the brain chip instantly. You can begin to play the game in less than a second.

Are Small Computers All Brain and Memory?

No. If they were, no one could use them. There must also be a way for you to *input* your information and orders to the computer. And a way for the computer to *output* its answers back to you. On a digital watch you input commands by pushing the watch's buttons. In this way you can set the time, set the alarm, or play the watch's built-in electronic game. The watch outputs its answer to you—the time or a game display—on a little screen on the top of the watch.

Inputting your orders to an arcade game computer is fun. You just push some buttons and move the control sticks back and forth. The computer outputs the results to the game's TV screen. You see alien space creatures getting zapped or purple monsters chasing little yellow-mouthed men.

Is There Any Way to Create Games of Your Own?

Not on digital watches, arcade games, or video games. But you can make up your own games on home computers.

Let's imagine that you are sitting in front of a small computer. It looks like a flattened typewriter wired to a TV and a tape recorder. You can create your own game by typing in commands written in a language the computer understands. Most small computers understand the BASIC (Beginner's All-purpose Symbolic Instruction Code) language, so the commands in our example will be in BASIC. There are, however, many other computer languages besides BASIC, just as there are many other human languages besides English.

TEACHING A COMPUTER TO PLAY A GAME

How Do You Teach a Computer?

You teach a computer by giving it a list of orders called a *program*. A computer teacher is called a *programmer*—a person who writes programs.

Who Was the First Computer Programmer?

The first programmer in history was Ada Byron (1815–1852), the daughter of Lord Byron, the famous poet. Ms. Byron was a very smart mathematician. She was also an interesting person. At parties she used to entertain guests by reciting multiplication tables while she played a fiddle and jogged around her family's billiard table.

What Computer Did Ms. Byron Program?

Ms. Byron was Charles Babbage's assistant on the Analytical Engine. Although Babbage's computer was never built, Ada Byron had already written dozens of programs.

What Kinds of Programs Did Ada Byron Write?

She made up several serious mathematical programs. She also invented a program to play chess and a program to predict the outcome of local horse races. This program was to win back the money she and Babbage had borrowed to build the Analytical Engine. At first the program worked. Then it failed. Predicting horse races was just too complicated. Babbage and Byron were chased around London by angry English bookies.

What Is Meant by a Bug in a Program?

It was easy to make mistakes when programming the Mark I, the world's first modern, electric-powered computer. When you gave the Mark I an order, it couldn't be in English. Instead it had to be in terms of the Mark I's thousands of electric *relays*. The relays were mechanical arms that turned power on or off in the Mark I's wires.

Grace Hopper, one of the Mark I's first programmers, tells a story about the first computer bug. One day the Mark I's programmers got an answer from Mark I that was obviously nonsense. They thought the answer was caused by an error in one of their programs. After careful study they learned that their program was okay but the Mark I wasn't.

The bad answer was caused by a dead moth stuck in one of the Mark I's switches. When the moth was removed, the program worked. Ever since then programmers who think they have a mistake in their program refer to the mistake as a *bug*. They say, "I have a bug in my program."

Were Later Computers Easier to Program Than the Mark I?

No. For example, take the ENIAC. The ENIAC was the world's first electronic computer. It used vacuum tubes instead of relay arms to route and magnify electrical charges. The ENIAC was very hard to program. It had almost no memory for storing programs. Instead, it had plugboards—big wooden boards filled with dozens of rainbow-colored, spaghetti-noodle wires. Each time you wanted to enter in a new list of commands to the computer, you had to pull the wires out of the old holes and plug them into new holes. It sometimes took a week just to program the ENIAC to solve a single problem.

Were Later Computers Easier to Program Than the ENIAC?

Somewhat, but not much. Later computers (in the 1950s and early 1960s) had much larger memories. You could type your orders to the computer on a typewriter and it would store the orders in its memory. On the other hand, all the orders had to be in the computer's special *binary* language of ones (1's) and zeros (0's).

Where Did the Computer's Binary Language Come From?

The language came from the way the computer stores and flashes electrical pulses. It doesn't matter whether the computer's circuits are made of relay arms, vacuum tubes, or tiny transistors. They all act like tiny light switches: they are either on or off. When they are on, the computer represents this with a "1." When they are off, the computer represents this with a "0."

With the early computers people had to write all their programs as enormous, caterpillar-like strings of ones and zeros. The string "0000000001001101" inside a computer, for example, might mean the number 77 or just the letter M. No wonder people found the early computers confusing!

Are Modern Computers Very Hard to Program?

Happily, no. Or else no one would use them.

In the mid-1950s scientists had a brainstorm. They figured, why make things so easy for the computer and so hard for people? Why spoon-feed the computer everything in its own language? Why not make the computer automatically translate people's commands into computer commands?

The idea worked. Since the 1950s scientists have developed new computer commands that are easier for people to use. The newest commands are not quite English, but they come close.

What Commands Do Computers Use Today?

Computers are like human beings. All human beings don't understand the same language. Some of us understand English, others Spanish, still others Chinese. The same goes for computers. Some computers understand BASIC, others Pascal, still others PILOT (Programmed Inquiry, Learning Or Teaching), Logo, or COBOL (Common Business-Oriented Language). Most small computers understand BASIC. That means they will obey commands in BASIC. Each computer language is made up of lots of different computer commands.

Do You Have to Be a Whiz to Program a Computer?

Many people think you have to be really bright in math to program a computer. This is just a myth. It is not true. Most computer commands in BASIC are English words (for example: RUN, PRINT, GET, PUT, and END). Most computer programs don't take any math skill at all to write. They just require some patience, some common sense, and a clear head.

But you do need to be careful what you tell a computer. It does exactly what you tell it—even if your commands are full of "bugs."

How Do You Write a Computer Game in BASIC?

Here's a game. All the commands are in the BASIC language. You type the commands into the computer one line at a time. As you are typing, each command appears on the TV screen connected to the computer's typewriter. At the end of each line, you push a button labeled "Return" to get the computer to store the line in its memory.

```
10 REM ••• MAKE YOUR OWN MONSTER •••
20 DIM A1$(20), A2$(20), A3$(20), A4$(20), A5$(20), A6$(3)
30 PRINT "I AM A MONSTER. WHAT IS MY NAME?"
40 INPUT A1$
50 PRINT "HOW TALL AM I (IN METERS)?"
60 INPUT A2$
70 PRINT "HOW MANY EYES DO I HAVE?"
80 INPUT A3$
90 PRINT "WHAT COLOR AM I?"
100 INPUT A4$
110 PRINT "WHAT DO I EAT FOR BREAKFAST?"
120 INPUT A5$
130 PRINT
140 PRINT
150 PRINT "HELLO, I AM "; A1$; " THE MONSTER."
160 PRINT "I AM "; A2$; " METERS HIGH."
170 PRINT "I HAVE "; A3$; " EYES."
180 PRINT "I AM AN UGLY "; A4$; " COLOR."
190 PRINT "IN THE MORNING I AM VERY HUNGRY."
200 PRINT "MY FAVORITE BREAKFAST IS "; A5$ ;"."
210 PRINT
220 PRINT
230 PRINT "DO YOU WANT TO MAKE A NEW MONSTER?"
240 INPUT A6$
250 IF A6$ = "YES" GOTO 30
260 PRINT "••• END OF MONSTER GAME •••"
270 END
```

How Do You Play This Game?

You simply type the word RUN, then push the Return button. The computer will obey each of the orders you give it, line by line. To play the game, you answer the computer's questions.

Let's pretend you have finished typing and storing the game in the computer's memory. You press RUN and the game begins:

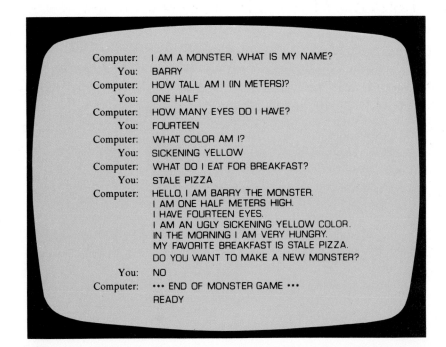

Computer:	I AM A MONSTER. WHAT IS MY NAME?
You:	BARRY
Computer:	HOW TALL AM I (IN METERS)?
You:	ONE HALF
Computer:	HOW MANY EYES DO I HAVE?
You:	FOURTEEN
Computer:	WHAT COLOR AM I?
You:	SICKENING YELLOW
Computer:	WHAT DO I EAT FOR BREAKFAST?
You:	STALE PIZZA
Computer:	HELLO, I AM BARRY THE MONSTER.
	I AM ONE HALF METERS HIGH.
	I HAVE FOURTEEN EYES.
	I AM AN UGLY SICKENING YELLOW COLOR.
	IN THE MORNING I AM VERY HUNGRY.
	MY FAVORITE BREAKFAST IS STALE PIZZA.
	DO YOU WANT TO MAKE A NEW MONSTER?
You:	NO
Computer:	••• END OF MONSTER GAME •••
	READY

39

How Do the Commands Work?

The first command (line 10) is a "dummy" command. It doesn't make the computer do anything. It's like a string tied around your little finger: It's a reminder note to *you* to tell you what the program does.

The second command (line 20) tells the computer to set up little memory cubbyholes to store your answers in. The cubbyholes are named A1$, A2$, A3$, A4$, A5$, and A6$.

The third command (line 30) tells the computer to type a question on the TV screen.

The fourth command (line 40) tells the computer to accept your answer to its question and store it in the memory cubbyhole you've called A1$.

Lines 50 through 120 are the same as lines 30 and 40—more questions and more answers.

Lines 130 and 140 print blank lines (to make things look nicer on the TV screen).

The monster introduces itself on lines 150 through 200. It mixes your answers in with its "canned" answers.

On lines 230 to 250 the computer asks you if you want to play the game again. If you answer YES, the computer hops back to the beginning of the game on line 30. If you answer NO (or anything else), the computer prints a final message, ends the game, and turns control back over to you. It finishes with a READY message. This means that it is ready to play the game again or learn a new game.

Can I Change the Program?

You sure can! A program is like a statue made out of wet clay. You can add to it, take parts of it away, or tear it apart and start over from scratch.

The Monster program above is the same. You can add new questions for the computer to ask or change some of the questions included here. The creature doesn't even have to be a monster. It could be a horse, a dog, or a pet turtle. You decide. As you change the program you will be learning how to teach the computer. When you finish, the program will be your very own—a product of *your* imagination.

THE COMPUTER GOES TO HOLLYWOOD

How Were Computers Pictured in Old Movies?

Just like they were in old stories and books—as big, bad, and unbeatable. For example, back in the 1950s Frederic Brown wrote a story about the ultimate computer. It was a giant computer made up of all the computers on the whole planet. When people switched it on, they asked it their toughest question: Is there a God? The computer replied, "There is *now*."

Most of the computers shown in the early books and movies were like Brown's giant computer. They knew everything. They didn't like people. And they wanted to take over the world. No wonder the average person thought computers were frightening and evil!

When Did This Movie Image of Computers Begin to Change?

In 1968 the movie *2001: A Space Odyssey* introduced a new superintelligent computer, the HAL 9000. In *2001,* unlike in earlier movies, human beings were not HAL's playthings. They were his masters. HAL was a tool of human beings. Yet he was also a tool that had gone bad. He was not all-knowing—a bug in his program made him go around murdering crew members on a spaceship. And he was not all-powerful—the last surviving crew member tricked HAL and pulled out his plug.

Can a Computer Really Be Evil?

No. Computers are like mirrors. They reflect us and our world. Our world is made up of good, evil, and a big gray area in between. Computers are taught by human beings. Most computers are used for good. But computers could be used for evil. It all depends on what their human masters teach them. Computers cannot do anything on their own.

Do Today's Movies Show the Good of Computers?

Yes. The older computers were rare, cost millions of dollars, and were programmed only by experts. The older writers and moviemakers didn't know any more about these old computers than the people who read their books and went to their movies. Now a new generation of small, easy-to-use computers has arrived. With it has come a new crop of young writers and movie directors. Many of them enjoy playing with video games. And they also use small, personal computers to help them with their work. They use computers to create special effects, cartoons, and many of the sounds and scenes in their movies. Some writers do much of their writing on computers. These new writers and directors are making computer movies that show the computer as it really is: a tool that gives answers—but not always the best ones.

Are Computers Being Used to Make Movies?

Yes. Computers are the hottest new moviemaking tool in Hollywood. One day soon computers will make it possible to create a whole movie without using film. Every sound and scene in the movie will be stored as trillions of tiny electric pulses inside the computer's memory.

How Are Computers Used to Make Movies?

Computers are used in many ways, yet most of them are invisible. Human artists teach computers to draw the fancy pictures and titles at the beginning of each movie. Computers create special sound effects and electronic music for movies. Many special effects are made with small plastic models whose movements are controlled by computers.

Thirty years ago animated movies and cartoons, like *Bambi* and *Snow White,* were made by dozens of artists who created every scene, every character, as still "paintings" on thousands of frames of film. When the frames of film were shown together rapidly, the characters came to life and seemed to move.

Today human artists are still creating animated movies and cartoons. But now computers are helping them.

Computers are also creating the scenery for movies with live human actors. The actors can do the scene on a darkened stage in Hollywood. Then the computer scenery is added. It might look like the actors are on one of Saturn's moons, in an ancient castle in Germany, or on a pirate ship sailing across the Atlantic.

Computers can be a mirror of our imagination. They are a way for us to take the worlds we create inside our heads and translate them into pictures and sounds we can share with other people.

With the aid of a computer, musicians can see the music they have composed.

COMPUTER-CONTROLLED ROBOTS

What Is a Robot?

A robot is any machine that has a computer for a brain and can move through or change the world around it. This means it must have arms, legs, wheels, hands, or something similar. There have been lots of clever, remote-controlled machines, but, until recently, no real robots. The invention of the computer made robots possible. And now that computers have shrunk to the size of an M & M, they fit inside a robot's body. Today there are thousands of robots in the world. They can perform tasks and answer questions. They still lack the ability to sense the world around them. However, a new generation of robots is now being built. These new robots have advanced computer brains and a limited ability to see, hear, touch, smell, and talk.

Hero I is a robot that can be assembled from a kit. It can detect light, sound, and motion, perform mobile tasks, and speak.

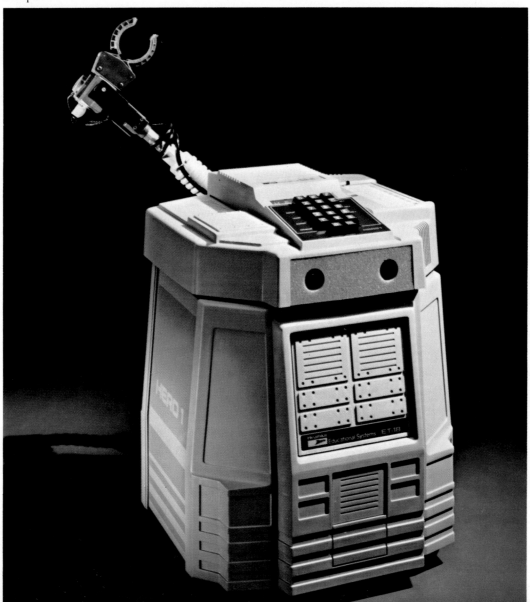

Are Robots in the Movies Real Robots?

No, not even R2-D2 and C-3PO. Movie robots are human beings wearing metallic costumes. Or they are life-size or miniature models made out of plastic and steel. The models move by remote control. Or people move the small models by hand. Using a technique called stop motion photography, they shift the arms and legs of the models a tiny bit at a time for each frame in a film. When the frames are flashed by at about twenty-four frames a second, the robots "come to life" and appear to move around on their own.

C-3PO and R2-D2 are not real robots. Actors are concealed inside of the metallic costumes, and sometimes R2-D2 moves by remote control.

Do Movie Robots Look Like Real Robots?

No. Movie robots often resemble human beings. Real robots rarely do. Most real robots look like a giant arm riding atop a trash can or fire hydrant. This arm is really robotic. At the end of the arm is a removable hand. Special-purpose hands can be attached to the robot arm to operate a power drill, a paint gun, or a welding torch. Scooplike hands can pick up heavy cartons and crates. Hooklike hands can dip a machine part into a bucket of molten metal. The robot may be able to see through electronic "eyes" that are mounted on its wrist. The eyes are really video cameras. The robot's computer brain is in its "tummy"—at the base of the arm.

A robotic arm replaces an assembly-line worker as it welds together parts of an automobile in this plant.

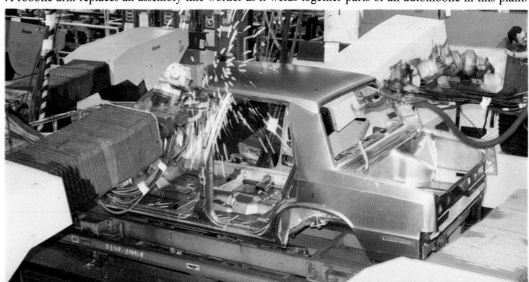

Do Movie Robots Act Like Real Robots?

Most old movie robots acted like old movie computers. They were supposed to be powerful superbrains who were evil or slightly crazy. Robots of this sort have been in the movies ever since the silent film *Metropolis,* back in 1927.

One of the first robots to appear as a human ally and tool was Robby the Robot in the film classic *Forbidden Planet,* made in 1956.

In recent movies robots are much more realistic. In the *Star Wars* movies C-3PO and R2-D2 seem to be computer controlled. They act like robots might someday act. And they aren't awful monsters. They are the good guys' friends and helpers.

Are All Real Robots Giant Arms?

No. Most factory robots are shaped like long arms because arms are the best-suited shape for assembly-line jobs like painting, lifting, and welding.

But a real robot can have any form at all. It can look like an arm, a dog, a mechanical man, a go-cart, a dinosaur, or an ashtray.

Can Kids Make Real Robots?

Yes. Lots of young people all over the world are making real robots. Their robots aren't robot monsters or robot maids or butlers. They are robot *pets,* like mechanical dogs, cats, and mice. The robots move on tiny rubber wheels, they obey spoken commands or whistles, and they are usually good at playing games. One robot even arm wrestles with its young inventor. All the kid-made robots look different, but many look like the favorite movie robot of all time—R2-D2.

After two passes through any maze, Moonlight Special, a robot mouse, learns the path perfectly. On the third run it maneuvers through the maze without making any wrong turns.

Can a Robot Pet Act Like a Real Pet?

Yes. Some kids have built robot turtles that scurry around the house. They beep and blink their eyes. And they draw pictures and shapes on the floor using a marker pen screwed into their tummy.

Robot dogs are very popular. One robot dog, Buster, is so smart that he can sense when his battery is low and he is "hungry." No matter where he is in the house, he begins to look for his "doghouse," where his battery recharger is located. He makes whining noises until he finds the recharger and plugs himself in. When he is "full" and his battery is recharged, he unplugs himself, yips happily, and begins exploring the house again.

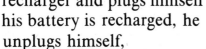

48

How Do Real Robots Help People?

Robot mice are being trained to explore underground mines and pipes and ductwork inside large buildings. Robot missiles can fly high in the sky like eagles, then dive down and destroy a tank on the ground. Robot airplanes can fly only a few feet off the ground, spy in enemy territory, and escape radar detection.

Robot arms and wheelchairs help handicapped people who cannot move. Robot space explorers are all over the solar system photographing the planets, moons, the sun, and occasional comets from deep space. Underwater robots can dive far deeper than human beings and help in undersea mining, farming, and recovery of lost ships. They also act as assistants to human divers and can help rescue divers who are in trouble.

How Do Real Robots Move?

By every way you can imagine—electric power, wheels, rudders, jet motors, tractor treads, and pressurized oil and air. A new generation of walking robots is now coming out of the laboratories. Some of these robots have as many as eight legs. (They're called *octopods*.) They can go places that are too rough and wild for other robots.

These new robots might be used to maintain an oil pipeline in a remote corner of the world. Or they might farm and mine the bottom of the oceans. Or they might ride atop a rocket. Or they might land on Mars or one of Jupiter's moons and explore its surface.

Will Robots Take Over People's Jobs?

They are doing that already. In Japan, the U.S., and Western Europe, robots are bumping human beings off assembly-line jobs. Robots cost less; they can work twenty-four hours a day, seven days a week; and they rarely break down. Human beings who lose their jobs to robots must be retrained, or else they will be unemployed.

Many people say we need robots to give our sluggish economy a big boost. They say that robots will eventually produce so much that we will all be able to take a permanent vacation.

But robots have other people worried. What happens in the meantime, they say, to all the people who lose their jobs to robots and can't be retrained or earn enough to support themselves and their families?

Nobody has a good answer to this question yet.

PUTTING COMPUTERS TO WORK

Can Handicapped People Use Computers?

They sure can! People who cannot speak are using small hand-held computers as electronic voices. When they press a button on the computer, it says a letter, a word, or an entire sentence aloud.

Computers inside typewriters are enabling blind people to learn how to type. When the person types a word, the computer pronounces it for him so he can make sure it is correct. And the computer automatically corrects commonly misspelled words.

Computers are helping deaf people talk on the telephone. Now, when deaf people call each other, they often use special computerized typewriters. One person types a message on her typewriter, then the message zips across the phone line and prints out automatically on her friend's typewriter.

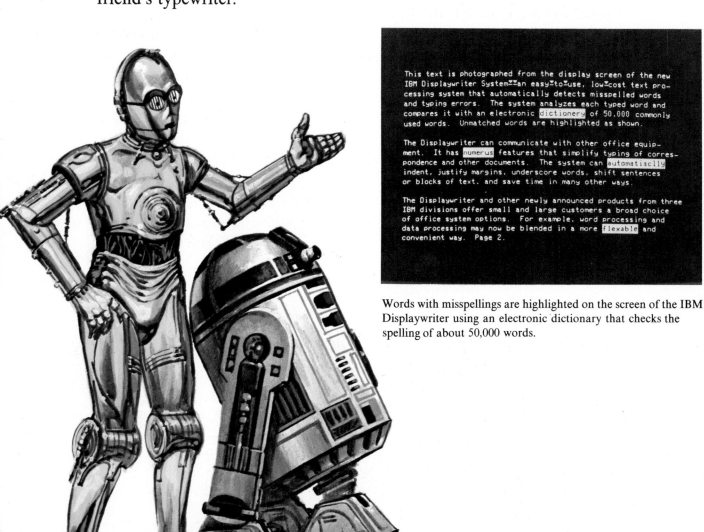

This text is photographed from the display screen of the new IBM Displaywriter System—an easy-to-use, low-cost text processing system that automatically detects misspelled words and typing errors. The system analyzes each typed word and compares it with an electronic dictionary of 50,000 commonly used words. Unmatched words are highlighted as shown.

The Displaywriter can communicate with other office equipment. It has numerus features that simplify typing of correspondence and other documents. The system can automatiaclly indent, justify margins, underscore words, shift sentences or blocks of text, and save time in many other ways.

The Displaywriter and other newly announced products from three IBM divisions offer small and large customers a broad choice of office system options. For example, word processing and data processing may now be blended in a more flexable and convenient way. Page 2.

Words with misspellings are highlighted on the screen of the IBM Displaywriter using an electronic dictionary that checks the spelling of about 50,000 words.

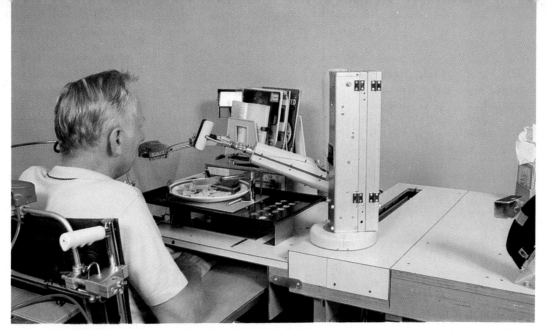

The robotic arm allows the user to select his next bit of food, delivers it to his mouth via eating utensils, then returns the utensils to the plate.

Can People Who Can't Use Their Arms and Hands Use Computers?

Yes. A new device called the OptoCom enables a person who has control of only his eyes to use a computer. A menu of letters appears on the picture screen. When the person stares at a letter, it is automatically entered into the computer. Using the computer, the person can switch on household appliances, make a phone call, learn the time, write a letter, and do many other things.

Other devices are just as amazing. One computer can be controlled simply by a person twitching his eyebrow. Another computer is controlled by its owner's toes. A robot arm has been developed at Johns Hopkins University that is controlled by a person's chin. The person can use the arm to feed himself, pick up the telephone, read a book, or play a game of cards.

This woman, whose arms are paralyzed, is able to use a typewriter at home with the aid of a device held between her teeth.

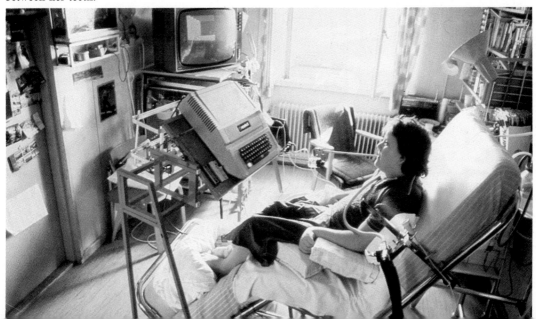

How Can I Put Computers to Work?

You can use a computer to help you do your homework—in math, history, music, art, or any other subject. You can write your book reports and stories on the computer picture screen. This lets you correct everything just by touching a few buttons. The final version, printed on the computer typewriter, looks like you had it typed by a secretary in an office.

You can also use a computer to help your family. One boy programmed poison antidotes into his computer. In an emergency a family member could type in the name of a poison and in seconds the antidote would appear on the screen.

Some kids go to work for their parents as part-time programmers. They write programs to help their mom and dad at home and at work, and they program games and educational programs for their younger brothers and sisters.

Lots of kids spend their time inventing computer games. Then they sell or trade these games to other kids.

As part of class projects, lots of kids are writing computer programs to help kids who are handicapped or who have trouble reading, writing, or learning in school.

A child sits at a home computer.

Can Teachers Use Computers in the Classroom?

Thousands of small computers are popping up in classrooms. Some teachers use a combination of small computers and small robots to teach their classes. At some schools the class project is to build a robot from a kit.

One school, in Pennsylvania, has several computers all wired together. The kids in the class sit in front of the computers and pretend that they are space cadets on a training mission in the Starship *Enterprise*. Their teacher has written several "mission" programs, including battles with enemy Klingon warships and exploration of mysterious new worlds. To have a successful mission, the kids have to work together as a team, think fast, and use knowledge they've learned in other subjects, like math, science, and music.

Where Else Are Computers at Work?

Almost everywhere in our society. Computers help pilot the Space Shuttle and guide the Shuttle's huge robot arm to lift satellites into orbit around the earth. Computers plan and schedule city buses. Computers automatically route telephone calls around the country and around the world. Computers help people make reservations on airplanes, trains, buses, and ocean liners. They look after stroke and heart attack victims in hospitals. They are used by musicians to help them compose new songs.

Astronauts use a team of on-board computers to pilot the Space Shuttle.

Can Computers Help Train Pilots and Astronauts?

Pilots and astronauts train to fly planes and spaceships by first "flying" in a computer-controlled cockpit. The cockpit looks like a real cockpit. However, instead of windows on its walls, there are computer TV screens. When the pilot or astronaut pushes a button or turns the steering wheel, the pictures on the TV screens automatically change. It looks like the person is really flying. But none of the pictures are real. They are all artificial images created electronically by the computer.

The computer can also put the pilot or astronaut through difficult drills. What happens if the ship's engines fail? What happens if a wing is sheared off? How does the pilot handle a fire on board his airplane, or a hurricane, or a fuel leak? The computer teaches the pilot or astronaut how to cope with emergencies, yet he or she never has to leave the ground.

Computer flight simulators teach pilots how to operate their airplanes, and astronauts how to control their spaceships.

Do You Have to Be a Businessperson or a Scientist to Use a Computer?

Not anymore. Twenty years ago only a few hundred computers existed, and they cost millions of dollars. Only businesspeople, scientists, and the military could afford them.

Today there are millions of computers that cost only a few hundred dollars. And some computers cost even less than a hundred dollars. They fit on your kitchen table. They use less power than an electric light bulb. Yet they are many times faster than the ENIAC, the grand-daddy of modern computers. So just about anyone can use a computer.

A dance teacher can use computers to plan out new dance steps. She can create a computer cartoon of little dancers whirling across her TV screen. Then she can rehearse the new step with her students.

A musician can program the computer to play music like a trumpet, a guitar, or a drum. He can rehearse a new song along with the computer. Then he can go out and "jam" with a live band.

An artist can use a computer as an electronic "sketchpad" or "paint-brush." She can draw on the TV screen with her finger or with a light pen wired to the computer. She can point to a menu of colors at the bottom of the screen (a "palette"), and the computer automatically fills in the picture with the colors she has selected.

COMPUTERS OF THE FUTURE

Will Computers of the Future Be Smarter Than People?

Computers of the future will become like human experts today. There will be computers who are experts in math, physics, game playing, medicine, and a thousand other subjects. But experts, despite their knowledge, don't always have the right answers. Their knowledge is limited. They may know a lot about their specialty (like nuclear power) yet little about the real world. This will be especially true about "expert" computers.

Computers of the future will not take over the world. They will still be tools. People will still be their masters.

What Will Future Computers Look Like?

Computer circuits (transistors and pathways) are shrinking fast. Back in the 1950s a computer with the same number of functions as the human brain would have filled the Empire State Building. And it would have taken Niagara Falls to power it. Today that computer could fit inside a TV set. By 1990 the computer will be smaller than the human brain and powered by a penlight battery.

If computer circuits keep shrinking, as scientists predict, by the 1990s we will have computers the size of notebooks and baseballs. Yet they will remember more information and be faster than today's supercomputers.

56

What Can a Computer Do Inside a Human Body?

Human bodies and computer bodies are similar in that both are "powered" by on-off electrical signals. Already people are using artificial computer-powered arms, hands, and legs. Other people are having operations that will put computer chips inside their bodies in order to regulate their heartbeats after a severe heart attack. Still other people are using computer chips in their ears to help them hear.

Some blind people are even using computer chips, implanted in their brains, to see. The chips absorb light and images, then bypass a person's sightless eyes and flash a "picture" directly to the person's brain.

In the future we may see computers implanted in people's throats. The computer will alter a person's voice to make it sound deeper, higher, more musical, or like the voice of the person's favorite movie star.

How Will We Give Orders to Computers in the Future?

To "talk" to a computer today, you need to know how to type. In the future, computers will have voices and "ears" and understand you when you speak to them out loud.

But we may not even have to talk to computers. Some scientists are now developing a way of tapping human brain waves so that they can turn a person's thoughts into electrical signals to the computer. Then, if we want the computer to do something, we will just have to *think* it. A computer will be like an electronic genie. "Your wish," it will say, "is my command."

Will Computers Ever Get So Advanced That They Become Alive?

Many computer scientists and experts on robots feel that what they are working on is *artificial life*. To them a computer or robot is like a primitive creature. The scientists are teaching this new creature how to see, hear, touch, smell, think, walk, and talk. Scientists say that it is like bringing a new baby into the world. The scientists think computers are like new babies, and we humans are the computer babies' parents.

Other scientists think that if computers ever do come alive, they will be so different that they will be like aliens from another planet. Their bodies (made out of silicon, plastic, and metal) are so different from the flesh-and-blood bodies we humans have. Also, computers think very differently than people do.

Other scientists disagree. They say that it's not important how computers are built. What is important is how they are programmed. We humans are the computers' teachers. We can teach computers to be playful, maybe even to have a sense of humor.

Will Computers Ever Think They Are Alive?

This is one of the biggest controversies among computer scientists. Some scientists say yes. Other scientists say no. These scientists say computers will never know they are alive. They say computers don't understand a single thing they do. They just blindly obey human orders.

A computer monitors the vital signs of patients in the intensive care unit of a hospital.

What Good Will Computers Do in the Future?

Most computers in the future will be used for good purposes. Computers will help doctors save lives. They will be the "eyes," "ears," and strong bodies for handicapped and elderly people. They will be used inside artificial limbs and artificial organs inside our bodies. They will help humans journey through outer space and underneath oceans. They may help us conquer diseases like cancer and unlock the secrets of the atom, gravity, and aging. Computer "experts" and intelligent assistants will help us do our jobs. They will teach us, befriend us, and help take care of us around the home. We will use them to play games, make movies and music, and draw beautiful electronic "paintings" on our TV screens. Computer-controlled robots will fight fires, defuse bombs, wash skyscraper windows, and do other hazardous work now done by human beings.

What Kind of Computer Jobs Will There Be in the Future?

Every kind. Everybody will be using computers in some way. You might become a doctor specializing in the use of computers in health. Or you may be a computer expert specializing in the use of computers in medicine. All fields will need computer experts.

Robotics, too, will be a good area for finding a job. Experts predict that the robot industry will eventually be as big as the automobile industry. Robots take people's jobs, but they can also make jobs. You can build robots, program robots, service robots, and design factories and offices where people can use robots.

Here are some exciting jobs you might consider: You might invent robot appliances that do work in the home. Or office robots that help people work. Or robot toys and robot "assistants" for kids and their parents. You might work with the police or FBI and use computers to solve crimes and catch criminals. You might help athletes train by using computers. Or use computers to analyze horse races, football games, or boxing matches. You might use a computer to write stories for electronic newspapers that appear on people's TV screens. You might use computers to entertain people: You could make computer movies, TV shows, games, music, and electronic books. Or you might invent an *expert system*—a smart computer that assists doctors or scientists. Or you might write programs for computers that teach and play with children.

You might be a computer-chip expert and design new kinds of computer-chips—music chips, picture-making chips, special chips to help robots "see" and "hear," superfast chips that can remember a library full of facts and figures, or chips that reason, think, and learn. Already, high school and college students are using intelligent computer programs to help them design new computer chips.

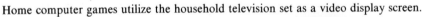
Home computer games utilize the household television set as a video display screen.

How Do Students Invent Their Own Chips?

Some young people say it is as easy as "painting by numbers." Others say it is like using building blocks.

First, the picture of an empty chip appears on the student's computer TV. She pushes some buttons and the computer fills in the empty spaces on the chip with pictures of transistors. The transistors and tiny electrical pathways soon fill the entire chip. Each pathway has a special color. The picture of the chip on the TV looks like a city street map. The streets are all the colors of the rainbow.

The student sends her chip picture to a chip manufacturer. A week later she gets her chip back. All the transistors, all the tiny pathways, are just like the ones on her TV screen. Only now they are real—and on a piece of silicon smaller than her fingernail. She can now plug her chip in and test it. Maybe it does something no one ever thought of before.

Making computer chips is a new frontier. Maybe you will become one of its first explorers.

GLOSSARY

binary language. The first language used by programmers to give orders to computers; consists of only ones (1's) and zeros (0's).

bug. A mistake in a computer program.

calculator. A special-purpose arithmetic machine that works with numbers but hasn't much memory. It is controlled by a computer chip.

chip. A silicon plate containing many transistors making up a logic circuit or a memory circuit.

circuit. Many transistors working together.

> **logic circuit.** Allows a computer to process information, do arithmetic, and make decisions.

> **memory circuit.** Stores programs and information.

computer. A machine that can store a huge quantity of information and be taught to perform an infinite number of tasks.

CPU (Central Processing Unit). One or more computer "brain" chips that, working together, process every order and every piece of information inside the computer.

dwarf computer. A computer that uses only one or two brain chips and a small number of memory chips. Dwarf computers are inside microwave ovens, electronic typewriters, digital watches, and video games.

program. The list of orders written in computer language and given to a computer.

programmer. A computer teacher who writes programs.

RAM (Random Access Memory). Memory chips that store all of the computer's current orders and information.

relays. Mechanical arms that control and route the flow of electrical power in an early computer.

robot. Any machine that has a computer brain and can move through or change the world around it.

ROM (Read Only Memory). Contains orders and information that cannot be changed, erased, or added to.

silicon. The special material in most transistors that conducts the flow of electricity from one pathway to another.

supercomputer. A classroom-sized computer made of hundreds of tiny computer chips all wired together.

transistor. The simplest computer pathway that carries, routes, magnifies, or stores charges of electricity.